A Conversation with Heinrich Franke

The West German Approach to Unemployment

Held on February 26, 1985
American Enterprise Institute for Public Policy Research
Washington, D.C.

ISBN 0-8447-3585-X

Library of Congress Catalog Card No. 85-061927

AEI Studies 428

85 - 1021 1

Printed in the United States of America

Foreword

The value of comparing public policies in the United States with those of other countries is that such explorations lend new perspectives to our own policy discussions and debates. This conversation with Heinrich Franke, cosponsored by the German Marshall Fund of the United States and AEI's Neighborhood Revitalization Project and chaired by Robert Pranger, director of International Programs at AEI, offers an opportunity for such a comparison.

Mr. Franke is president of the West German Federal Employment Institute, a "corporation under public law" directly associated with the federal government but federally supervised only to the extent necessary to ensure the institute's observation of the law. Supported by contributions from employees and employers, the Federal Employment Institute is responsible for setting labor market policy in West Germany as well as for managing related activities designed to maintain the equilibrium of labor market supply and demand. Vocational guidance, placement of apprentices, public job placement services, promotion of vocational training and retraining, job creation and maintenance, and the payment of unemployment benefits and assistance are all duties of the institute.

This autonomous institution conducts its functions independently of the federal government and is self-governed at the central, regional, and local levels by appointed representatives from employee, employer, and public bodies. Each of these three partners is equally represented in number and power and thus contributes equally to the policy development process.

In his recent book, *Presidential Economics*, Herbert Stein, AEI senior fellow and former chairman of the President's Council of Economic Advisors, comments that a major barrier to better economic development policy in the United States is a political one: because it is mainly politicians who set the tone and practice of economic policy in this country, short-term policies serving special interests too often take precedence over long-term policies that would better serve the national interest. Even when intellectually capable and sophisticated politicians and government bureaucrats make the decisions, personal or regional considerations outweigh the national interest. Stein contends that private people are closer to and thus more knowledgeable about economic conditions and opportunities and therefore have better knowledge of where resources should go.

Stein also points out that relying upon voluntary cooperation by business and labor is often ineffective. He notes that the distinction between government mandates and "suggestions" when dealing with problems involving government, business, and workers is a weak one: "However initially determined to keep the system voluntary, the government cannot remain uninvolved if its suggestions are conspicuously disregarded by business and unions . . . the government invariably is drawn into using other influence to 'persuade' businesses or unions to comply."

These observations by one of America's most respected and experienced economists suggest that the U.S. approach to labor market policy could be improved by some sort of a policy-setting structure that draws business and labor into the policy-making and implementation process at an early stage. This structure would encourage close cooperation between government, business, and labor, as well as create a formal opportunity for private people to add their better information to the policy development and implementation process. West Germany enjoys such a structure in the form of the Federal Employment Institute.

As Mr. Franke points out in his remarks, the control of unemployment is an urgent issue in both the United States and West Germany, but practical ways and means for dealing with it and related issues are subject to wide differences of opinion. Policy makers and analysts in the United States in recent years have been exploring ways of creating better public-private partnerships. This conversation adds to the body of knowledge and may offer practical ways and means that can be adapted to the American experience.

WILLIAM J. BAROODY, JR.
President
American Enterprise Institute

Introduction

Heinrich Franke, who is president of the Bundesanstalt für Arbeit, the West German Federal Employment Institute, speaks to us here on the importance of employment policy to international economic competition. This session was one of the American Enterprise Institute's series of conversations with distinguished visitors. We would like to acknowledge our gratitude for the support of the German Marshall Fund in collaborating on this presentation. We have worked in the past with the German Marshall Fund in various other programs on the French economy, on environmental policy, and on U.S.–Italian economic cooperation. We welcome again this opportunity to join with the German Marshall Fund.

Before a formal introduction of Mr. Franke, a few words may be in order about the work of the American Enterprise Institute in the fields of social policy and America's competitive status in a changing world economy. Since the early 1970s, this institute has been involved in innovative research in social policy, beginning in the field of health policy. This is now a very large project at this institute, under the direction of Dr. Jack Meyer and his senior associate, Sean Sullivan.

Since 1975 we have expanded our research in education, in welfare, in law enforcement, and in housing. Among AEI's projects is the Neighborhood Revitalization Project, which cosponsored this conversation with the German Marshall Fund. The Neighborhood Revitalization Project, under the direction of Cicero Wilson, examines U.S. social and economic policy in key urban centers of the United States. It gives special emphasis to the ways of creating better public-private partnerships and encouraging private entrepreneurship.

This institute is also very much involved with government regulation policy under the general direction of Dr. Marvin Kosters. Our periodical *Regulation: AEI Journal on Government and Society* deals with this subject. We are very concerned about the impact of government regulation and other government projects and policies on productivity and employment in our country. We have established a special

1

project on America's competitive position in the changing world economy, which looks at trade, education, and hi-tech policies in the United States. We note the importance of education policy in the work of the West German Federal Employment Institute, which is, of course, involved not only with unemployment insurance, a historic pioneering policy of modern Germany, but also with public placement service, vocational guidance, and promotion of vocational training.

Heinrich Franke is president of the West German Federal Employment Institute. He has been a member of the West German Parliament since 1965 and served as chairman of the Christian Democratic Union's Parliamentary Group on Labor and Social Affairs. Since 1984 he has been president of the Federal Employment Institute, one of the world's most sophisticated public agencies responsible for labor market policies. The agency is governed by a tripartite board, including representatives of employers, employees, and government.

Mr. Franke grapples with many of the problems that confront U.S. policy makers, problems of unemployment, training, retraining, and job placement and of maintaining the equilibrium of labor market supply and demand. All of these issues are as urgent in the United States as in Germany. These issues are of concern to policy makers of both nations as they consider ways to maintain the skilled work force necessary to support a strong economic position, both domestically and internationally.

In recent years American government at all levels has turned to the private sector for assistance with employment issues. These initiatives, which are still under way, have achieved varying degrees of success.

The Federal Republic of Germany, through the Federal Employment Institute, enjoys a unique level of cooperation between employers, employees, and government. How that cooperation is achieved and how much effect it has on labor market decisions are matters of great interest to American decision makers.

So we at the American Enterprise Institute, in collaboration with the German Marshall Fund, are indeed fortunate to present this conversation with Heinrich Franke. In it he explores and allows us to explore with him German strategies for dealing with labor market policy in the international context.

ROBERT J. PRANGER
American Enterprise Institute

2

A Conversation with
HEINRICH FRANKE

The West German Approach to Unemployment

I am happy to have the opportunity to discuss problems of the labor market in the Federal Republic of Germany, in particular the role the Federal Employment Institute is playing in the German labor market. Of course, my remarks are made from a European perspective. Like all other Western industrialized nations, Germany has been struck by its worst labor market crisis since World War II. This crisis had several causes, which had different weight in the various countries, though they all contributed to it. They include the deep economic dips, especially those resulting from the two oil price explosions; the structural shifts; and the enormous rise in the supply of wage and salary earners as a consequence of the baby boom, in the beginning of the 1960s.

If I were to offer only one explanation together with one theory based on it, I would be limiting myself without contributing much to the solution of labor market problems. We are probably all agreed on one point: Unemployment on the scale seen in the Federal Republic and the Western World in general is the main sociopolitical challenge of the 1980s. No one involved in the labor market can escape it— neither the employer nor the employee nor the government or its institutions. Nor can other societal groups, such as political parties, churches, and trade associations, afford to remain aloof.

In this connection, the catchword of an employment pact offers itself. Control of unemployment is certainly recognized as the first priority, but opinions differ widely as to the practical ways and means. One thing is certain: There is no panacea; there is no royal road to a solution. What we need is a set of measures, a path of many steps.

Each of these little steps will have only a limited effect, but the sum total can develop a considerable impact. For me, priority number one is increased economic growth. Economic growth may not be everything, but without economic growth, everything else is in vain. Only a healthy economy can in the long term safeguard work places and create new ones.

We can probably agree on a second point as well: Growth alone will not solve our employment problems. Again, this point is made in the light of German conditions. With all other conditions unchanged, that would require a real growth of 5 to 6 percent annually over the long term, and that is an optimistic estimate. No matter how much we hope, we will not achieve it; therefore we need a comprehensive employment and labor market policy as an undergirding.

In my talk I would like to limit myself to labor market policy. The law has imposed this task upon the Federal Employment Institute as its foremost concern.

We work under a law—the so-called act to stimulate employment—that is the guideline for our labor market policy action. It requires the Federal Employment Institute to implement measures within the framework of social and economic policy of the federal government in such a way that the high level of employment is achieved and maintained, that the employment structure is constantly improved and thereby the growth of the economy promoted.

This first paragraph contains two targets—one dealing with quantity, "the high level of employment," and one with quality, "the improvement of the employment structure." Both are intended to serve economic growth. In so doing, the law makes it clear that labor market policy, like all other political areas, cannot operate in a vacuum. It is determined by a wealth of underlying conditions and influencing factors. I would like to touch only upon economic, fiscal, educational, and wage policy. In the last analysis, however, no political area is unconcerned with employment nowadays. I mention this in order to caution against expecting an expansionary labor market policy to carry the main burden in controlling unemployment.

With the funds and means provided by the act to stimulate employment and to work on labor market policy, at most 15 to 20 percent of registered unemployment could be absorbed or placed. Nevertheless, one should not underestimate the contribution of a labor market policy as a safeguard against unemployment. I would express it this way: With the aid of fine-tuning it supplements the more global measures of a general employment policy by the federal government, and in so doing it fulfills an indispensable function. As examples, I would like to describe a few of the basic tasks of labor market policy being carried out by the Federal Employment Institute.

The institute's principal policy is that precaution is more important than relief. Prevention comes before therapy. In other words, by preventive measures, employment conditions are maintained, work places are stabilized, and employees receive from the start the necessary support. Social security funds are spent only in the event of loss of a work place.

An important task of the Federal Employment Institute is to gather comprehensive information on the working world. Information is a labor market policy tool whose long-term and in-depth effects can hardly be overestimated. Whoever in politics or in the economy needs to make decisions that have a cyclical or structural impact needs reliable information on the job market. The same is true for those engaged in labor negotiations, the representative of social security, and, finally, the general public, which has a vital interest in the labor market and in the development of careers.

In its Institute for Labor Market and Career Research, the Federal Institute has created for itself a remarkable research and information potential. Such information is indispensable in counseling those at the crossroads between a general and a professional career or at the transition point from vocational education to a first job or at a change of career.

Another service available at the Federal Employment Institute is job placement, an essential part of its task. In achieving an equilibrium between work-place supply and demand—qualitatively as well as quantitatively—the Federal Institute acts as a mediator and as a broker in balancing the interests of the employer and of the employee. On the one hand, it channels suitable workers, and, on the other, it helps to find an adequate work place. In so doing, it must consider that each employee has a personality of his own and his own capabilities, attitudes, desires, and lifestyle. It also has to consider that each employer has specific requirements and special demands. It must attempt to consider both the employer and the employee in following the principle of placing the right man or the right woman in the right work place.

At present, the large job deficit makes placement difficult. In January 1985 unemployment amounted to 2,619,000, or about 10.6 percent of the total. The high number of unemployed and the much smaller number of open positions makes equilibrium impossible.

The Federal Employment Institute tries to provide suitable workers as soon as possible for open positions, and it can do so more easily now than ever before because of the high number of unemployed. The mediators try to establish close contacts with employers, and they use public relations to get more positions listed with the institute. The introduction of modern methods, such as computer-aided job placement, should achieve even faster placement, better communications, and more rational organization.

Professional or vocational qualifications are decisive in determining the chances of individual job seekers in the labor market, but they also have an importance beyond the individuals. In the last analysis they also determine how far the highly industrialized national economy will develop. Not only are basic scholastic or vocational training important; continuing education also becomes urgent in adapting to structural and technological change.

The Federal Employment Institute considers the promotion of occupational training, continuing education, and retraining the centerpiece of an active dynamic labor market policy. Vocational training and professional qualification may not offer absolute protection against unemployment or inadequate employment, but whoever has completed a professional education, who is mobile professionally, and who is ready to add constantly to his store of knowledge will be much less threatened by unemployment and will be easier to place than the unskilled worker.

I would like to mention two further tools by way of an example—short work, and job creation. Over the past two years especially, short work has proved itself as a preventive labor market policy. It comes to play mainly during a phase of cyclical uncertainty. If an employer's orders decline, he would have to reduce his work force. For one part of the work force this would mean unemployment. To maintain employment, however, the entire work force can temporarily reduce its work time. In that case the loss of earnings will be made less serious by short work benefits, paid by the employment offices. In this way, an employer can keep his well-trained permanent staff. Of course, this reduction must be temporary: we must never try to keep obsolete organizations alive with short-term benefits.

Work relief measures are another means of stabilizing the labor market. Grants may be awarded to promote work in the public interest that otherwise would not be performed at all or would be performed only at some later time.

Such measures must be appropriate to a labor market policy point of view and give work, at least temporarily, to a certain number of unemployed people. For other employees, such as the permanent staff of the concerned firm or the supplier companies, these measures often mean the maintenance of their work places. The government and social security receive taxes and contributions from these workers, and the labor administration need not pay them unemployment benefits. In this way, unemployment is avoided, at least for a while. Many people can keep up with developments in their own profession or regain skills or acquire additional qualifications. Such measures must remain temporary, of course; they cannot be allowed to substitute for permanent, profitable, and promising work places.

Sometimes, however, unemployment cannot be avoided, either by relief, training methods, or other means of controlling the labor supply or by an expansion or maintenance of employment. Then, as the last resort, wage substitute benefits become necessary, and unemployment benefits are paid.

Under the Act to Stimulate Employment, the Labor Administration is responsible for all phases of the working life and all connected social security measures. This coordination has proved to be a great advantage—one not enjoyed in many other countries.

The measures required to provide protection and to safeguard workers against unemployment has, of course, influenced the organization of the agency charged with these tasks. Therefore the German Labor Administration is not organized like other social security branches. In 1927, an organization was created to give uniform insurance to all employed persons in the area of the former Reich. After World War II, this type of organization was maintained in the conviction that only a nationwide agency could deal with such tasks.

I would like to stop my remarks at this point to answer any questions you may have.

I would also be happy to hear suggestions from you on how you can help us or how we can work together in tackling these problems. Thank you.

Questions and Answers

REESE HAMMOND, International Union of Operating Engineers: A paper prepared for the Manpower Services Commission of the United Kingdom, addressing apprenticeship in the Federal Republic, stated that, of the total youth input, about 10 percent dropped out, 20 percent went on to higher education, and 70 percent entered some kind of dual education, including apprenticeship. And of the 70 percent who entered dual education, only 5 percent dropped out. Now, that is a phenomenal record of maintaining students in skill training, and I wondered if there was some secret that you could hand out to us.

MR. FRANKE: I believe there is no real secret to it. At present, we have a big problem as a result of the high birth rates of the baby boom years. We now have many persons ready to enter either higher education or the dual system of vocational training and apprentice-ship education. In the economy, we are now seeing a slight turn around but no real recovery as yet. This combination of circumstances has presented particular difficulties, since not every youngster can go on to higher education. During the past fifteen years, there has been a sort of euphoric feeling that everybody who wanted to go to a university could go. But now we are seeing a number of dropouts and underachievers who want to come back and get commercial training or acquire a craft or a trade because they feel that way they will make a better livelihood. They aggravate our problem of placing youngsters. Otherwise the secret of our success is only the challenge it has constituted for our system.

JANET NORWOOD, Bureau of Labor Statistics: It certainly is true that demographic factors are now less favorable to fuller employment in Western Europe than in the United States. Nevertheless, I have the impression from discussions with representatives from Germany and other Western European countries that they rely to a rather large degree on job sharing and shorter work hours, rather than on job creation. Is there a danger, do you think, that this rather pessimistic approach to the problems of the future will continue?

MR. FRANKE: I see the economy showing a real growth of between 2.5 and 3 percent this year and possibly 2.5 to 3 percent in the

8

following year. Of course, this depends on world trade and on the strength of the U.S. dollar. If the economy should continue normally, and if we should have gone over this demographic hill and continued toward the valley, then I believe the whole situation will reverse itself. At the beginning of the 1990s, we will observe a lack of workers because it is a statistical fact that whoever has not been born cannot work. Therefore we should begin thinking about investing more in the brains of our young people and not deal with the problems only with a pessimistic approach. Of course, there are politicians who might like to emphasize that approach, but I feel that the young people and the society are well able to cope with them.

Did I understand your question correctly, Mrs. Norwood? Did I answer your question?

Ms. NORWOOD: You did answer it in part. The concern that I expressed was related more to the next few years and to the focus of discussions with many Western European people on work sharing and shorter work hours, rather than on the creation of new jobs. That is a matter of some concern to me.

MR. FRANKE: Yes, this was the second part of your remarks and I should like to answer. You mentioned the two things, job sharing and short work. Short work refers to someone who remains at his work place but works less. There is quite a discussion going on in Germany about the 1 million to 2 million people who would not mind working less than the usual nine hours per day. They would be happy with part-time or short work. We are trying to take care of them, to create the social security framework for them to have all the necessary safeguards under such an arrangement. Other European Community countries are trying to go in a similar direction.

There are also cyclical changes and structural changes. I personally feel that Europe lags in not recognizing these changes early enough and that we have to catch up in order to be able to compete with other nations, especially with Japan. But this requires a long-term effort.

MR. PRANGER: There is still the issue of new jobs. Do you mean new job creation when you talk about long-term development? Is your Employment Institute involved with new job creation?

MR. FRANKE: Job creation measurements are a solution for times of unemployment, especially high unemployment. With an average of 2.2 million unemployed, 80,000 new jobs—and this is the number of new jobs—represents a drop in the bucket. This cannot solve the problem.

I am certain that future plans will deal with the service sector, because in industry many jobs have been lost over the past few years. I am thinking of steel and of shipbuilding and of agriculture. In 1950, 25 percent of the employed people in Germany worked in agriculture. Today less than 6 percent do, and I believe 3.9 percent do in your country. In 1970, in Germany 700,000 people were employed in the mining industry. Today the number has shrunk to 160,000. So you see, this is a structural change. If the economy had been favorable, there would have been no difficulty in absorbing these workers, but it was unfavorable, and therefore the problem was aggravated.

SAR LEVITAN, George Washington University: I would like to follow up on Dr. Norwood's question. Since the commissioner of labor statistics talked about philosophy, I would like to talk about a few numbers, just some specifics.

In your presentation, which was a very, very informative one, Mr. President, you gave us a good idea of what the Federal Employment Institute does, the principles on which it operates, and how it creates policy for the German Republic. My question is, How much money do you actually spend on job creation, and on tender orders, and can we then compare that with what we do in the United States? I wouldn't be surprised if we might learn something from Germany, rather than your learning something from us. I suspect that you haven't given us the numbers, that you are really doing a great deal in job creation, and that this also reduces a great deal of unemployment. I also suspect that what you spend on vocational education and on the apprenticeship program far exceeds what we are doing and that you therefore may have a much better prepared labor force than we have in the United States.

MR. FRANKE: Our budget is 33 billion German marks, which comes from contributions in equal parts from employers and employees. Our overall budget actually amounts to 58 billion because the law also gives us responsibility for the payment of child allowances, for bankruptcy losses, and for job creation measures in times of emergency. This year we will spend 3.8 billion German marks for job creation. Other measures are continuing education, retraining of workers, and all the efforts connected with the labor market policy. They will total 7 billion German marks. I could give you a long list, professor, if you wish, of what this comprises.

Now, in regard to short work relief, I told you that job creation methods cost 3.8 billion German marks. We also make relief payments in case of short work to make up for loss of income. We have a special program where people can retire early, from fifty-eight years on, and special measures come into play in that case. These programs amount to 5 billion German marks.

KITTY HIGGINS, Senate Labor and Human Resources Committee: Can you tell us what percentage of unemployed workers are participating in these various programs—that is, how many are in short work week, how many are participating in job creation, and how many are in retraining? I think your statement indicated that these workers are not just getting income transfer but in fact were in these programs. Would you be a little more specific on that?

MR. FRANKE: I would like to clarify that all who participate in retraining programs, training and education programs, short work relief, or job creation programs are not counted in the unemployment statistics, because they are working. They are not counted as unemployed.

As far as eligibility for retraining or job creation measures are concerned, we take the people who are hard to place, the handicapped people, and young people who have not yet paid into this system but should be able to benefit from placement or continuing education and retraining. We work with the young and the handicapped, and we sometimes achieve miraculous results. We train them for sophisticated machinery, like automated lasers, so that they later can be placed easily.

I said before that with the aid of our measures, between 15 and 20 percent of the unemployed are benefited. We also estimate that during the course of this year, because of our labor market efforts, another 320,000 people will be benefited who do not appear in the unemployment figure because of training and the like.

WILLIAM KOLBERG, National Alliance of Business: I have a very straightforward question, but it might require a long answer. What would be missing if the private partners weren't involved in the operation of your agency but only the government?

MR. FRANKE: Well, half of our contributions come from employers, but I think your question is much more far-reaching—What do business and industry do as regards continuing education and training and retraining of workers?

If we did not plan and did not have their cooperation, the

problem would be aggravated. Then it would become a political problem. I feel this cooperation is sound social policy and sound politics, especially for a nation situated at the crossroads to nations of a very different philosophy. Thus for us it becomes a moral and ethical obligation.

Now, as far as the role of the employers in our institute is concerned, we did not need to force them or to exercise any persuasion. They represent one-third of the members of the supervisory board.

ANNE HEALD, German Marshall Fund: To follow up on the previous question on the role of the employers and of industries in the training system in Germany, I know in our country many questions are being asked about the kind of training and education needed for the future. Is business raising those kinds of questions about the training system in Germany now?

MR. FRANKE: The question as to the best way to train workers is not raised much by business and industry representatives. In years past it has been a topic for the political parties. The type of training played a role, but it is no longer so topical now.

The question as to the best education and training system really cannot be answered.

MR. PRANGER: Mr. Franke, we would like to thank you for making this presentation at the American Enterprise Institute. We find it very important in our work at AEI to compare various approaches to social policy between the United States and other countries. We appreciate that the Federal Republic of Germany has a very special social philosophy—which is basic to the federal constitution—in this compact between employers and employees, one meant to develop social harmony and peace in the postwar period in West Germany. And we appreciate your being here to discuss with us this very significant social experiment and also to look at the future of this policy in West Germany.

Thank you again.

MR. FRANKE: I would like to thank you for having treated me so kindly. And by way of conclusion, I would like to say that social stability has a political effect. We believe that social stability can maintain government stability. Because of our social stability, we were able in the postwar period to regain an entry into the Western nations. To maintain this stability is in our mutual interest.

12